ADRIANA LUNA CARLOS
Editor-In-Chief, Designer and
Co-Founder

HANNA OLIVAS
Managing Editor & Co-Founder

FENIX INNOVATION
MAGAZINE

SHE RISES
STUDIOS

ADVERTISING OPPORTUNITIES
Info@SheRisesStudios.com

FENIX INNOVATION *MAY 2024*

CONTACT US
SheRisesStudios@gmail.com
www.SheRisesStudios.com

www.SheRisesStudios.com

LETTER FROM THE EDITORS

Dear Readers,

Welcome to the May 2024 issue of FENIX Innovation Magazine! As we delve into the vibrant world of digital media and arts, we're thrilled to present a lineup of captivating features, insightful interviews, and expert perspectives aimed at igniting your imagination and fueling your creativity.

In this edition, we're honored to feature Marissa Warren on our cover, a beacon of inspiration in the realm of business transformation. Marissa's article delves deep into the subconscious mind, unveiling the secrets to rapid business evolution. Prepare to embark on a journey of self-discovery and empowerment as Marissa guides us through the intricate process of aligning our conscious and subconscious minds for unparalleled success.

But that's just the beginning. Throughout this issue, you'll encounter a wealth of content designed to elevate your experience and expand your horizons. From exploring the convergence of artistry and technology to diving into the world of gaming and entertainment, there's something for every enthusiast within these pages.

As we celebrate the luminaries of the arts and honor excellence in creativity, innovation, and storytelling, we invite you to join us on this exhilarating journey where technology meets imagination. Together, let's push the boundaries of what's possible and dare to dream big. Thank you for being part of the FENIX Innovation community. Your passion and curiosity inspire us to continue pushing the envelope and exploring the uncharted territories of the digital arts.

Enjoy the May 2024 issue, and may it ignite your creativity and spark new ideas that propel you toward your dreams.

Warm regards,

Adriana Luna Carlos and Hanna Olivas
Editors of FENIX Innovation Magazine

HOW TO CREATE RAPID TRANSFORMATIONS IN YOUR BUSINESS

Marissa Warren

Do you ever wonder how some people seem to have rapid success in their business? Meanwhile, you feel like you have tried everything and your progress is at a stale point. You can't seem to break past a certain point. Your income never goes over a certain level or you only ever get the same number of clients or sales.

There could be more going on under the surface than you realise. Your subconscious could be out of alignment to your conscious mind and creating self-sabotages or limiting beliefs – even though you are not aware that these are happening. This is why resolutions don't work…. You think you will get up early before work to go to the gym, or you tell yourself that starting Monday you are on a diet, but then that time rolls around and you have a million reasons why you can't do it. Consciously you know you want change, but subconsciously you are being kept stuck and in a comfortable, familiar place, even if that is not where you want to be. You have to get the two minds synchronised and in alignment with each other.

The conscious mind is the voice in your head that you are aware of. I call this the loud mind and is the part of your mind that you directly experience and can control. This is your awareness, decision-making, short-term memory, communication, self-reflection and time perception. This shapes your experiences, behaviours and interactions with the world around you.

The subconscious mind is the part that operates below the level of conscious awareness. This is the silent mind and the one that operates and controls you, your thoughts and actions on auto pilot. Your thoughts, feelings and memories live here. 90% of your operating systems are controlled by your subconscious mind and when you are working at this level, this is where change comes from. When you work in the subconscious, it is rewiring your neural pathways to bring your conscious and subconscious mind into alignment to help you break free from inner limitations and move into the life you want to be living.

Real change and rapid transformations come from bringing the conscious and subconscious mind into alignment with each other. By reforming and creating new neural pathways, you are opening up new ways of thinking and rewriting your belief systems. Many of your beliefs are not yours alone and have been formed throughout your lifetime and by those around you.

Doing the subconscious work is the magic tip to being able to move from where you are to where you want to be, without the overwhelm and by making change easy.

If you were to look at your life and business, can you see repeated patterns playing out over and over again? Do you feel like one area of your life is amazing, while another is struggling? Part of doing the subconscious work is taking aligned action to move you in the direction you want to be moving in. To first be able to do that, you need to get clear on where you are and where you want to go. It's time to tune in!

Follow these journal prompts below to start to gain some clarity in your life and business and to identify the future version of you that is already living the life you want to be living.

- What thoughts does the future me think?
- How do they show up in the world daily?
- What does their life look like?
- Are you fulfilled in your work?
- Is this your soul's purpose and passion?
- You have solid daily rituals to help keep your mind, body, energy at a certain level
- Are all areas in equilibrium? Mental, emotional and physical health
- You have quality relationships with your family and friends
- These connections and relationships fulfilling and supportive
- Do you feel seen, heard, valued and accepted as you are?

Lean into this and keep pushing through if any discomfort arises. This is the area that the biggest growth comes from. This can give you insights and answers into some of the reasons why you are doing the things that you are doing.

Diving into the subconscious work is one of the best gifts you can give yourself! Working with someone like myself that can tap directly into your subconscious is one of the best ways to fast track this work. I can access deeper parts within yourself and find the blind spots that you may not be able to see yourself.

If you would like to chat about how I can help you to access your subconscious to help you break free and move forward in life to where you want to be, in the fastest amount of time possible, please book a free discovery call. Looking forward to connecting with you. Scan the QR code below and book a time.

🌐 www.marissawarren.com

📷 www.instagram.com/marissawarren_

📘 www.facebook.com/marissa.warren.transformational

🔗 www.linkedin.com/in/marissawarren-hypnotherapist- transformationalconsultant/

BUILDING COMMUNITY, INSPIRING CONFIDENCE: JASNA'S IMPACT IN THE BEAUTY WORLD

In the bustling world of beauty, Jasna Bukvic Bhayani stands out not just for her skillful hands but for her heart-driven approach. Passionate about connecting with women on a deeper level, Jasna's journey in the beauty industry began with a desire to empower and uplift others. Over time, her commitment to enhancing natural beauty and cultivating inner confidence has only strengthened.

Jasna's journey into the beauty industry was ignited by her innate desire to connect with like-minded women and empower them to feel their best. She finds joy in nurturing individuality and authenticity, believing that true beauty lies in embracing one's uniqueness. As she honed her skills, her passion evolved into a mission to celebrate and enhance the natural features of her clients, rather than conforming to societal standards.

One poignant moment that solidified Jasna's dedication occurred during a transformative session with a client. Witnessing the newfound confidence and self-love radiating from her client's transformation reaffirmed Jasna's commitment to her work. It was a testament to the power of embracing one's true self and the impact it can have on one's life.

In her daily interactions with clients, Jasna embodies her philosophy of enhancing natural beauty and celebrating individuality. She listens attentively to her clients' preferences and insecurities, tailoring her services to accentuate their inherent beauty. By creating a space that honors individuality and self-expression, Jasna empowers her clients to confidently embrace their true selves.

Running Contour Institute Makeup Artistry Skin & Lasers involves a delicate balance of client care, business operations, and personal fulfillment. A typical day for Jasna is a dynamic blend of providing personalized services, managing administrative tasks, and fostering a warm, inviting atmosphere. Through effective time management and clear communication, she ensures that each client receives exceptional care while tending to the operational aspects of the business. This balance allows her to derive personal fulfillment from every interaction, knowing that she is empowering individuals to embrace their beauty and confidence.

Establishing a sense of community among her clients is paramount for Jasna. Through client events, workshops, and personalized follow-ups, she creates a supportive and inclusive environment where individuals can connect, share experiences, and uplift each other. Jasna believes that community plays a crucial role in self-care and beauty, offering a platform for encouragement, inspiration, and camaraderie. Through community, clients not only receive beauty services but also find a supportive network that enhances their self-care journey and reinforces their sense of empowerment and confidence.

In essence, Jasna Bukvic Bhayani's journey in the beauty industry is a testament to the transformative power of embracing one's true self and celebrating individuality.

CONNECT WITH JASNA

 www.facebook.com/DreamLashStudio

 www.instagram.com/contourinstitute_

 +1 (704) 681-1509

 www.contourinstitute.com

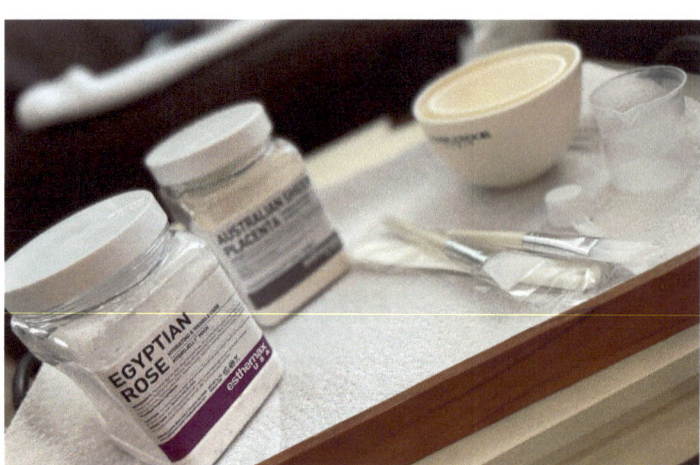

BY JASNA BUKVIC-BHAYANI

PERFECTION

by Debra Hillard

One of the things about hiding ourselves is that we're afraid to appear human and vulnerable. We think that we have to have it all together before we allow ourselves to be seen. Well, I am too old to wait any longer. I'll never have it all together, nor do I aspire to that anymore. Appearing perfect is exhausting and it doesn't allow for our humanity. It doesn't allow for others to be human around us. All it does is put up walls.

If aging has taught me one thing, it's that I have little to no control over the passage of time and the effect that has on my body. There is no way to grow old and maintain any semblance of perfection, at least by our society's standards. I used to hide because I believed that I wasn't good enough to be seen, that I was so flawed that it was best to remain behind the curtain and give the limelight to those who deserved it. The beautiful ones, the successful ones, the "perfect" ones, the ones who seemed to have that magic something that we all aspired to.

Growing up in the decades that I did, the images of women that I was supposed to aspire to were airbrushed models, frighteningly thin, with no expression on their faces. They were mannequins, not humans. I was supposed to be quiet and not make waves. Not think too deeply or challenge those in charge. Keep my dreams, my opinions and my desires to myself to appear acceptable, especially to men. If I wasn't perfect enough then no one would want me. It wasn't who I was that was important. t was what I looked like to others that told me whether I was *"perfect"* enough. I never felt like I had it all together. Never felt acceptable enough, lovable enough. I was one of those people who might have appeared to have myself together, but that was merely a facade to mask just how "not together" I actually was. I learned early on that survival meant appearing a certain way and became a master at appearances.

Holding up a facade becomes exhausting and doesn't allow for the actual experience of living. I had to lose my facade piece by piece, over years of illness and debilitation, to finally come to where I am now. Real. Flawed. Human. And ultimately perfect at being ME.

"Perfectly imperfect" is what I like to say about myself. There is no reason to hide away anymore, thinking that somehow, one day, I would be acceptable enough to show my face. No, my face is what it is. It shows my age and experience, my wisdom and heartbreak. It shines with the resilience I've developed over a lifetime of being knocked on my ass and getting back up aga

I'm like an old tree who has weathered more storms than I can count, but is still standing, broken limbs and all. Where I've been broken, I've grown back stronger. Every scar is a mark of my strength to persevere. And each wrinkle on my body marks the passage of years learning how to be fully myself. Now those are attributes worthy of celebration, not hiding. Those are the things about me that connect me to every other human on the planet. We are all just humans trying to live our best lives with the imperfections we have, baring the scars we bear. It doesn't make us less worthy or ugly or unacceptable. It simply makes us human.

WOMEN ON THE
Rise

Unleashing the Power Within:
Self-Discovery and the Pursuit of Greatness

by Stacey Dori

In a world where we are constantly bombarded with external influences and societal expectations, the challenges of having the perfect body, or lavish lifestyle, it is easy to lose sight of our true selves. However, the journey of self-discovery and the pursuit of greatness holds the key to unlocking your fullest potential. It is through understanding who we are at our core and embracing our unique qualities that we can embark on a path of personal growth and ultimately achieve greatness.

Finding the strength to love yourself or embrace who you are or who you're becoming is a very essential part in learning more yourself through activating your. strength. Understanding our strengths helps us channel our energy into areas where we excel, leading to a greater sense of fulfillment and triumph. During our journey of self-discovery, we must also acknowledge our weaknesses that allow us to identify areas for growth and development, enabling us to overcome obstacles and reach new heights.

Along this process, it is ok to be vulnerable, or to embrace vulnerability. Vulnerability will allow us to open ourselves up to new experiences, perspectives, and opportunities for growth. Showing Vulnerability doesn't imply that you are weak, it shows that you are willing to identify the areas in your life that need attention. Letting your guard down will allow us to be authentic to who we are becoming. The journey of self-discovery and the pursuit of greatness are intertwined journeys that empower us to tap into our true potential. It is important to create space for personal alteration for the breakthrough of your true potential. Let go of fear and doubt and embrace all the greatness the universe has in store for you. You are becoming the best version of yourself, and there is no limit to your success.

✉ staceygarel@gmail.com　　　f stacey2qute

Embracing Innovative Leadership: A Personal Journey

By Kimberly Seabrooks

As I reflect on my journey as a leader, I realize that embracing innovative leadership has been both a challenge and a reward. Leading with innovation is not just about adopting new technologies or implementing creative strategies; it's about fostering a culture of continuous improvement, adaptability, and visionary thinking. This personal perspective offers insights into what it means to be an innovative leader and the impact it can have on an organization.

Embracing Visionary Thinking

From the outset, I understood that having a clear, forward-thinking vision was crucial. Early in my career, I noticed how quickly market dynamics could shift and how businesses that failed to anticipate change often lagged behind. Determined not to fall into that trap, I made it a priority to stay informed about industry trends and technological advancements. By doing so, I could set a vision that not only prepared my team for the future but also inspired them to strive for it. One of the most transformative moments in my leadership journey was when we decided to pivot our company's focus towards sustainable practices. At the time, it seemed like a risky move—an uncharted territory filled with uncertainties. However, by articulating a clear vision of how sustainability could differentiate us from competitors and appeal to a growing segment of eco-conscious consumers, I was able to rally my team around this bold new direction. The results were beyond our expectations, leading to increased customer loyalty and opening new markets.

Empowering My Team

Empowerment has always been a core tenet of my leadership philosophy. I believe that the best ideas often come from those on the front lines. Early in my tenure, I established an open-door policy and encouraged team members to share their ideas and feedback without fear of reprisal. This culture of openness not only fostered innovation but also built trust within the team. One initiative that stands out was the introduction of our "Innovation Fridays," where employees could work on projects of their choosing. This not only boosted morale but also led to several breakthrough ideas that we eventually implemented. By trusting my team and giving them the autonomy to explore, we created an environment where innovation thrived.

Navigating Challenges with Adaptability

Adaptability is another hallmark of innovative leadership. The business world is inherently unpredictable, and the ability to pivot quickly in response to new information is essential. I've faced numerous situations where our initial plans had to be discarded in favor of more agile approaches. Each time, the key to success was maintaining flexibility and encouraging my team to view challenges as opportunities for growth. During the global pandemic, we were forced to rethink our operations entirely. Remote work, digital transformation, and shifting consumer behaviors all posed significant challenges. By fostering a mindset of adaptability, we not only managed to sustain our operations but also discovered new efficiencies and opportunities that will benefit us long after the pandemic subsides.

The Impact of Innovative Leadership

The impact of innovative leadership on our organization has been profound. We've seen enhanced performance, with our productivity and revenue metrics consistently exceeding targets. Employee engagement and satisfaction have soared, as team members feel valued and motivated. Our commitment to innovation has also positioned us as a market leader, attracting top talent and establishing strong industry partnerships.

Reflecting on my journey, I am convinced that innovative leadership is not just a strategy for success but a necessity in today's dynamic business landscape. It requires visionary thinking, empowerment, adaptability, and a relentless pursuit of improvement. By embracing these principles, I have not only guided my organization towards achieving its goals but also fostered a culture where innovation is ingrained in our DNA. In conclusion, the path to innovative leadership is challenging but immensely rewarding. It demands courage, foresight, and a willingness to trust and empower others. As I continue to lead, I remain committed to these ideals, confident that they will drive our sustained success and growth in the years to come.

 kimberly.seabrooks    @healthcoachkim    channel/UCMMPM

SRS ACADEMY
EMPOWER**HER** HUB

She Rises Studios (SRS) Academy is a groundbreaking online platform exclusive to online educators catering to women entrepreneurs. Our mission is to empower women worldwide through high-level skills courses and workshops that cover a wide range of topics essential for personal growth, career advancement, and business success.

LEARN MORE

SheRisesStudios.com/srs-academy

From Corporate to Entrepreneurship: Journey of Reinvention

by Alicia Fuentes

Straight out of university, I embarked on a career in the corporate world, driven by a burning desire to make a meaningful impact in the field of Health, Safety, and Environment. Little did I know that this journey would span 28 years, marked by numerous trials and triumphs that would shape me into the person I am today.

Alicia Fuentes

As a woman navigating the male-dominated landscape of my industry, I faced my fair share of challenges from the outset. Yet, armed with determination and a relentless pursuit of excellence, I forged ahead, determined to carve out my place in the corporate hierarchy. Despite my introverted nature, I understood the importance of stepping out of my comfort zone, seizing every opportunity to gain exposure and refine my skills.

However, along the path to success, I encountered moments of profound self-doubt and self-criticism. There were times when I questioned my abilities and even sabotaged my own progress. Without the guidance of mentors to illuminate the way forward, I relied on sheer grit and resilience to navigate the treacherous waters of corporate life.

Through the ups and downs, I gleaned invaluable lessons about the power of embracing change and the necessity of staying true to oneself. Each setback became an opportunity for growth, each obstacle a stepping stone towards personal and professional development.

But perhaps the greatest test of my resilience came when I received the unexpected news of my redundancy and subsequent retrenchment from my job. It was a devastating blow – one that shook me to the core and forced me to confront the harsh realities of corporate loyalty. I found myself at a crossroads, unsure of what the future held.

In the depths of despair, I realized that I had a choice – to succumb to the weight of disappointment or to rise above adversity and forge a new path forward. Drawing upon my faith and inner strength, I made the courageous decision to chart a course of my own making, one that would lead me towards a life of purpose and fulfillment.

For years, a buried desire for coaching had lingered within me, whispering of untapped potential and unfulfilled dreams. With newfound determination, I seized the opportunity to pursue this passion wholeheartedly, enrolling in courses and seeking guidance from seasoned professionals who shared my vision.

The journey was not easy – it required sacrifice, dedication, and an unwavering belief in myself. Yet, with each passing day, I felt myself growing stronger, more confident, and more aligned with my true purpose. Through the support of my newfound community of coaches and mentors, I honed my skills, defined my niche, and crafted a magnetic message that resonated with others.

Today, I am living proof that resilience knows no bounds and that reinvention is always within reach. I have traded the confines of the corporate world for a life of autonomy and fulfillment, surrounded by like-minded individuals who inspire me to reach greater heights.

To anyone struggling with unfulfillment or uncertainty, I offer this advice: Take the time to embark on a journey of self-discovery, reevaluate your intentions and goals, and eliminate limiting beliefs that hold you back. Trust in the power of the Universe and never underestimate your own potential to create the life of your dreams.

In conclusion, my story serves as a testament to the transformative power of resilience, reinvention, and unwavering faith in oneself. As I continue on this journey of growth and discovery, I am reminded that the greatest adventures often begin where comfort ends – in the vast unknown of possibility and potential.

 Empower Her: Igniting Transformation through Sisterhood

 Alicia Fuentes

FROM STRENGTH TO STRENGTH: THE IMPORTANCE OF FEMALE EMPOWERMENT

The power of female empowerment and women working together is truly inspiring. When women unite and uplift each other, we create a force that can break down barriers and overcome stereotypes that hold us back. The strength that comes from female empowerment is contagious, as it builds resilience in women and encourages us to push for our best selves.

But the benefits of female empowerment go beyond individual success. When women have equal access to resources and opportunities, we can make a significant difference in the world. We can become leaders, innovators, and changemakers who shape the world for the better. Our contributions can bring about positive change in society, helping to create a more equitable and just world.

One of the most important aspects of female empowerment is its impact on future generations of women. When young girls see strong women in leadership positions and succeeding in their careers, they are inspired and encouraged to pursue their own dreams and aspirations. They begin to believe that they too can achieve greatness and contribute to society in meaningful ways.

The benefits of female empowerment are numerous, from economic growth to improved mental health outcomes. For instance, advancing gender equality could add $12 trillion to the global GDP by 2025. By supporting and empowering women in the workplace, we can create a more prosperous and inclusive society. Women's groups have been instrumental in fighting for women's rights and gender equality, leading to significant changes in laws and policies that have made the world a better place for women.

When women work together, they become an unstoppable force. Women are known for their resilience, hard work, and determination, and when they join forces, they become even more powerful. By creating a supportive environment where everyone can thrive, women can share their experiences, knowledge, and resources with one another, and help each other achieve their goals. Working together also allows women to pool their resources and expertise. For example, women who are starting businesses can join forces to share their knowledge and experience. This can help them avoid common pitfalls and increase their chances of success. Women can also pool their resources to fundraise for important causes or to support other women who are struggling.

When women go after their goals with intention and support, they can achieve anything. And achieving those goals can lead to positive changes in society's attitudes toward women. When women are seen as equal and respected members of society, it sets a positive example for future generations. By breaking down gender stereotypes and challenging harmful beliefs, we can create a more just and equitable world for all.

It's crucial to remember that female empowerment is not a one-size- ts-all solution. Women come from diverse backgrounds and face unique challenges. Therefore, it's crucial to build a network of support that is inclusive and supportive of all women, regardless of race, ethnicity, sexual orientation.

As we work towards female empowerment, let's celebrate and embrace the truth that strong women elevate each other. When we come together and support each other, we can achieve incredible things and create a better world for everyone. Let's continue to inspire and empower each other, and let's work towards creating a world where women are valued, respected, and celebrated.

www.innerstrongfitness.com | www.advancedmedicine.ca
www.facebook.com/nicole.arseneau | www.facebook.com/2innerstrong | www.instagram.com/innerstrong

Elevate your brand through creative and impactful content!

EMPOWER**HER** CONTENT DAY

SEPTEMBER 21, 2024 | LOS ANGELES, CALIFORNIA

EmpowerHer Content Day equips attendees with the tools and knowledge needed to craft compelling content for social media, podcasts, and videos.

DRIVING FUTURE HIGHWAYS

As our world becomes increasingly digital, industries are racing to incorporate the latest technological marvels. One area experiencing a significant paradigm shift is the auto industry, thanks to the advent of blockchain technology and Non-Fungible Tokens (NFTs). If these words sound like gibberish, hold tight! By the end of this journey, we'll understand how these innovations are driving us towards a disruptive and thrilling future.

Blockchain, NFTs, and What They Mean

First, let's decode the jargon. Blockchain, essentially a public ledger, is a chain of blocks where each block contains information. The technology is transparent, tamper-proof, and provides a perfect platform for creating trust in a trustless environment.

NFTs, on the other hand, are unique digital assets that use blockchain technology to prove their authenticity and ownership. They're like digital collectibles - only one true version exists, and the blockchain can confirm who owns it.

The Intersection of Blockchain, NFTs, and the Auto Industry

The auto industry, like any other, thrives on innovation. With the integration of blockchain and NFTs, we are witnessing significant changes in ownership models, supply chain management, and even the very concept of cars.

The Case of Revo Motors

Consider a hypothetical company Revo Motors, a trailblazing automaker, that has just unveiled its new line of electric vehicles (EVs). These aren't just any EVs, but vehicles integrated with blockchain technology, utilizing NFTs in several groundbreaking ways.

1. Vehicle Ownership and NFTs: Each Revo vehicle is associated with an NFT, which serves as a digital certificate of ownership. The NFT contains all the necessary information about the car, including its manufacturing details, maintenance records, and ownership history. This feature could revolutionize car resale, making the process as simple as transferring a digital token.

2. Supply Chain Management: Revo uses blockchain to manage its supply chain. Parts used in the cars have corresponding digital tokens, offering transparency, traceability, and efficiency in the production process. This system drastically reduces counterfeit parts and ensures quality control, leading to safer and more reliable cars on the road.

3. Vehicle Customization: Here's where it gets really cool! Revo has created an ecosystem where customers can purchase NFTs representing custom parts and enhancements for their vehicle. Want a new sound system or a more powerful battery? Buy the corresponding NFT, bring your car to a Revo service center, and voila! Your vehicle is upgraded.

Driving Towards a Greener Future

The hypothetical business Revo Motors is just one example of how blockchain and NFTs can reshape the auto industry. Blockchain's potential to improve supply chain efficiency not only reduces costs and ensures quality, but also contributes to sustainability. Transparency in the supply chain allows for responsible sourcing of parts, reducing environmental impacts.

Moreover, NFT-based ownership models could encourage shared mobility solutions. Imagine a future where you own a percentage of a vehicle as an NFT. This model could provide the flexibility of using a vehicle when you need it without the need to own it entirely - a shared, decentralized approach that would reduce the number of vehicles produced and, consequently, our carbon footprint.

As We Park the Conversation

Blockchain and NFTs are steering the auto industry into uncharted territory. With potential benefits such as transparency, enhanced ownership models, and efficient supply chains, these technologies promise to reshape our concept of vehicle ownership and usage.

Buckle up, folks! The road to the future of the auto industry is being paved right before our eyes, and it promises to be an exciting, revolutionary ride. The digital revolution isn't coming; it's already here, making the auto industry more secure, efficient, and environmentally friendly. And with these exciting innovations, who knows what the next exit on this highway holds? We would love to hear your thoughts or questions about this technology

Written By:

Lauren Weiss

+1(316)530-1142

www.cyclealign.com

hello@cyclealign.com

LIFESTYLE & *Wellness*

MEET SHANNON SALGE

1. Can you share with our readers a brief overview of your entrepreneurial journey? What inspired you to start your own business, and how did you overcome initial challenges?

I have always had a passion for health & fitness! But after being a manager at a gym for a few years, I realized that women weren't getting all the help I felt they deserved or needed in a traditional gym setting. I wanted to build a business that helped women not only with nutrition & training, but also with functional lab testing, mindset work, and a different level of accountability. One of the initial challenges was people thinking that in-person coaching was the way to get them to their goals best. But after clients spend a few weeks in our program, they appreciate our holistic viewpoint on their health journey and how much quicker they see progress!

2. Many aspiring entrepreneurs struggle to scale their businesses to six figures and beyond. What key strategies or tactics did you implement that you believe were instrumental in achieving this level of success?

The first thing I did when I wanted to start my own company was hire a business mentor. I think if you truly want to succeed, and succeed quickly, invest in yourself to learn from people that have done it before you. Secondly, make sure you are in a business that you truly have a passion for. It's easy to get burned out, but when you love what you do day in and day out, you can't help but keep striving for success.

3. Building a strong brand and online presence is crucial in today's digital age. How did you develop and promote your brand to attract high-paying clients or customers?

Showing up regularly and confidently on social media is key nowadays. I love talking about my program and all the amazing client transformations we've had. But honestly, more importantly, I have loved providing free education and value to the people that consume my content.

4. As an entrepreneur, one often faces setbacks and obstacles. Can you share a significant hurdle you encountered along the way and how you managed to navigate through it?

Yes, I think this is inevitable, but helps you grow stronger as an entrepreneur! In my first year in business, I spent a lot of time trying to hire team members to help me grow. But, sometimes the first people you hire aren't going to be the people that line up with the future vision of your business! So I think firing my first two people and spending a ton of time finding the right fits for those positions (and then hiring another 2 more) was the hardest, but best thing that has happened! Spend the time trying to nd the right ts on the front end and take the time to train them properly. It's time well spent that will pay you back tenfold.

5. Women entrepreneurs often encounter unique challenges in the business world. What advice do you have for other women aspiring to reach six-figure success in entrepreneurship and overcome gender-related obstacles?

Be unapologetically YOU. Entrepreneurship is already draining enough, so don't waste your time trying to be someone that you are not. Spend time honing in on your craft, became damn good at what you do, and people can't help but be attracted to you no matter what.

www.facebook.com/shannon.salge
www.facebook.com/groups/1298733640503815
www.instagram.com/shannonsalgetness

Bridging the Gap Between Personal and Professional Development

A Journey of Resilience, Triumph, and Breaking Barriers in Science and Technology

Written By: Adriana Reid

Life has a remarkable way of challenging us with adversity, and my story is a testament to the power of resilience and hard work. From being an immigrant single mother of three who fled my country amidst a forced migration due to a bad marriage and corruption, I have defied stereotypes to become an international speaker, author of "Decoding Corporate Wellness and Performance through Human Software Reprogramming" (awarded as #1 New Releases on Amazon), and entrepreneur in the field of personal and professional development. As a woman who forged her path in STEM-related fields, I understand the unique challenges faced by women in these careers. This article chronicles my transformative journey and how I now empower women in STEM to bridge the gap between personal and professional growth

A Journey of Resilience

The path to where I stand today has been marked by unwavering determination. Raising my children almost entirely on my own among the difficulties of being an immigrant single mother was no small feat. My ex-husband's being in politics became a blessing and a curse; he found every loophole to evade child support obligations after a turbulent divorce. However, my commitment to creating a better life for my children fueled my drive for success and ignited a passion for empowering others to overcome their own adversities.

An Integrative Career Path

Equipped with a master's degree in education, I embarked on a journey to the United States in 2008 to work with veterans, helping them recover from PTSD symptoms using transcendental meditation techniques and pioneering in the field of Human Software Engineering. My experience as a diplomat, wearing various hats as a cultural and press attaché, Consul for tourism and community affairs, allowed me to significantly impact my country's international relations. Yet, when I left the service, I felt a calling and concluded: there is a gap between personal and professional development, who we are as human beings, and what we do to get what we think we need. This led me to a profound realization about the suffering that often arises in this space.

Launching Be2Be-Coaching, Inc.

In 2021, I embraced a new chapter in my life by founding Be2Be-Coaching, Inc. The inspiration behind my company came from recognizing the need to align personal values with professional aspirations to promote a thriving workforce. My company serves as a bridge, providing personal development training to executives and C-suite professionals to create awareness and empower individuals to overcome their challenges.

When I became a translator between personal development and STEM Language

Growing up in a conservative value-oriented family, my father's profession as a Civil Engineer significantly influenced my early life. I always had a keen interest in human development and the transformation of unconscious patterns that caused unnecessary suffering. I recognized the need to translate my expertise in human development into a language that my father, with his STEM background, could understand and resonate with.

Empowering Companies Through Neuroscience

Incorporating knowledge from exceptional teachers and my personal experiences, I developed a methodology that invites companies to align their staff's values with the company's mission and vision. Utilizing neuroscience-based technology, we empower individuals by teaching them how their minds and brains function, enabling them to embrace their full potential through self-discovery.

As a woman who has experienced her share of challenges in STEM-related fields, I am deeply committed to empowering other women to shatter stereotypes and achieve greatness in their careers.

Through Be2Be-Coaching, Inc. we create awareness for personal and professional growth. Together, we rewrite the narrative for women in STEM, empowering them to reach their full potential and embrace their passions fearlessly. As we continue on this empowering journey, we pave the way for a more inclusive and innovative future in the exciting world of science, technology, engineering, and mathematics. As I continue to make a positive impact on the lives of others, I am grateful for the opportunities that have shaped me into the person I am today.

6-Figure AUTHOR

Ready to turn your passion for writing into a thriving 6 figure income 🪐

Join the exclusive "6 Figure Author" program and unlock the strategies and support you need for unparalleled success!

SIGN UP NOW

GOOD THINGS COME TO THOSE WHO HUSTLE

A mother of three, real estate team leader, speaker and entrepeneur, Peggy Pratt has never taken the easy road. Growing up in the city of Boston, Peggy was exposed to a diverse group of people and business owners who mentored and impulsed her into the business world. Her strong work ethic and motivation pushed her forward and multiple businesses later, she discovered that real estate was her thing. She loved communications but found that the money part was difficult, so she gave up on the radio program. The restaurant business was lucrative, but she still felt something was missing. Real estate was the one place she knew she could make a difference in a family's life, while building her own portfolio and securing her financial future.

She was fortunate enough to meet mentors, such as her for her brokers, along the way that guided and supported her. She began building her real estate portfolio, flipping, buying, selling and holding onto rental properties. Through the years, she raised her family with her husband and traveled the world. Peggy states "To me, one of the best gifts I can give my children is the gift of travel and education. I will also give them the tools to fend for themselves but not hand outs" Her oldest, Joshua has just graduated as a Plastics Engineer from Umass Lowell. Her daughter Sophia will be headed to Providence College this fall to study medicine. Her pungent JJ is going to be a junior in high school and already works in the construction field like his dad.

As far as her career goes, Peggy has been involved in multiple boards including being Past President of the Lynnfield Rotary club, Past President of the Nahrep Boston chapter and currently a National coach for them (an organization she loves and is very involved with) and is currently a board member of the Massachusetts Housing Coalition and the Realtors MLS Pinergy website. She believes being involved and giving back is extremely important.

Through the years she knew she couldn't handle the business alone and formed a small team which is comprised of newer agents that she has fostered and trained. Like her own children, she personally feels responsible for bettering their lives and future. The Pratt Properties team in currently #55 in the nation on the National Association of Hispanic Real Estate agents 2023 list and #3 Century 21 team in Massachusetts.

As far as her personal life, she is selling her very large home in the suburbs and is moving to a smaller home back in the city that she purchased when she was just 21 years old. Downsizing and moving after her recent divorce , she says is "opening new doors for more travel and a lighter financial burden which will allow me to stop and smell the roses at my 47 years of age" Peggy is extremely excited for this new chapter in life and is living it to the fullest.

Todo es Posible:

4 Lessons From a First Generation Lawyer's Journey

By Zoila M Gomez

In the realm of real-life fairy tales, a young girl's dreams don't always revolve around castles and princess. Zoila Gomez, a proud Latina immigration lawyer and founder of Gomez & Palumbo Law, dared to dream of a life beyond the confine of her humble beginnings. Her journey from a picturesque village in the Dominican Republic to advocating for those who lack a voice Is a tale of perseverance, opportunity, and empowerment. Here are four invaluable lessons we can glean from her remarkable journey.

Lesson 1: The Power of Self-Discovery

Zoila's story is one of self-discovery fueled by her early exposure to stories of hope and wonder. Growing up in the vibrant countryside of the Dominican Republic, she found solace in books and the radio, igniting her imagination, and instilling in her the belief that life held endless possibilities. Her realization that she could rise above her circumstance and shape her destiny became the cornerstone of her journey, showing us that the first step toward transformation lies in recognizing the power within ourselves.

Lesson 2: Finding your Voice Amidst Adversity

Even amidst the serenity of her village, Zoila's early life was marked by challenges. As a child, she experienced bullying and derogatory name-calling, which ignited her determination to stand up for herself. It was her mother's words, "Take the broom and beat them with the stick", that set her on a path of self-empowerment. Embracing the power of her words, Zoila learned to assert herself, ultimately transforming her vulnerability into strength. Her journey teaches us that adversity can be a catalyst for discovering our voice and harnessing its power.

Lesson 3: Embracing Change and Overcoming Limitations

At the age of eighteen, Zoila embarked on a new chapter in the United States, armed with determination and a thirst for learning. Undaunted by the challenge of mastering a new language, she wholeheartedly embraced the process of learning English. Her journey from waitress to confident communicator showcases her unwavering commitment to self-improvement, highlighting that change and growth are achievable when met with resilience and unyielding spirit.

Lesson 4: The Transformative Power of Education

Education became Zoila's beacon of hope and transformation. Fueled by her desire for better opportunities and a better future for her son, Zoila embarked on an educational journey that defied all odds. From ESL classes to a bachelor's degree and ultimately, law school, she exemplified the tenacity required to break barriers and transcend limitations. Zoila's journey underscores the transformative power of education, reminding us that pursuing knowledge can pave the way to new horizons.

Life has a remarkable way of shaping individuals, molding them into strong, resilient beings capable of overcoming even the most challenging circumstances. Zoila Gomez's journey from a modest village in the Dominican Republic to becoming a pioneering lawyer and advocate speaks to the universal themes of resilience, empowerment, and the pursuit of dreams. Her story teaches us that amidst adversity, we can find our voice, empower ourselves, and rewrite our destinies Through change, learning, and determination, Zoila's life serves as a testament to the truth that "Todo es possible" – everything is possible.

www.facebook.com/zoila.m.gomez | www.linkedin.com/in/zoila-gomez-6b910620
www.zoilagomez.medium.com | www.gomezpalumbolaw.com

FENIX TV

NEVER MISS A MOMENT OF YOUR FAVORITE SHOWS

Watch on any device! Fenix TV is available to watch on all major devices and operating systems.

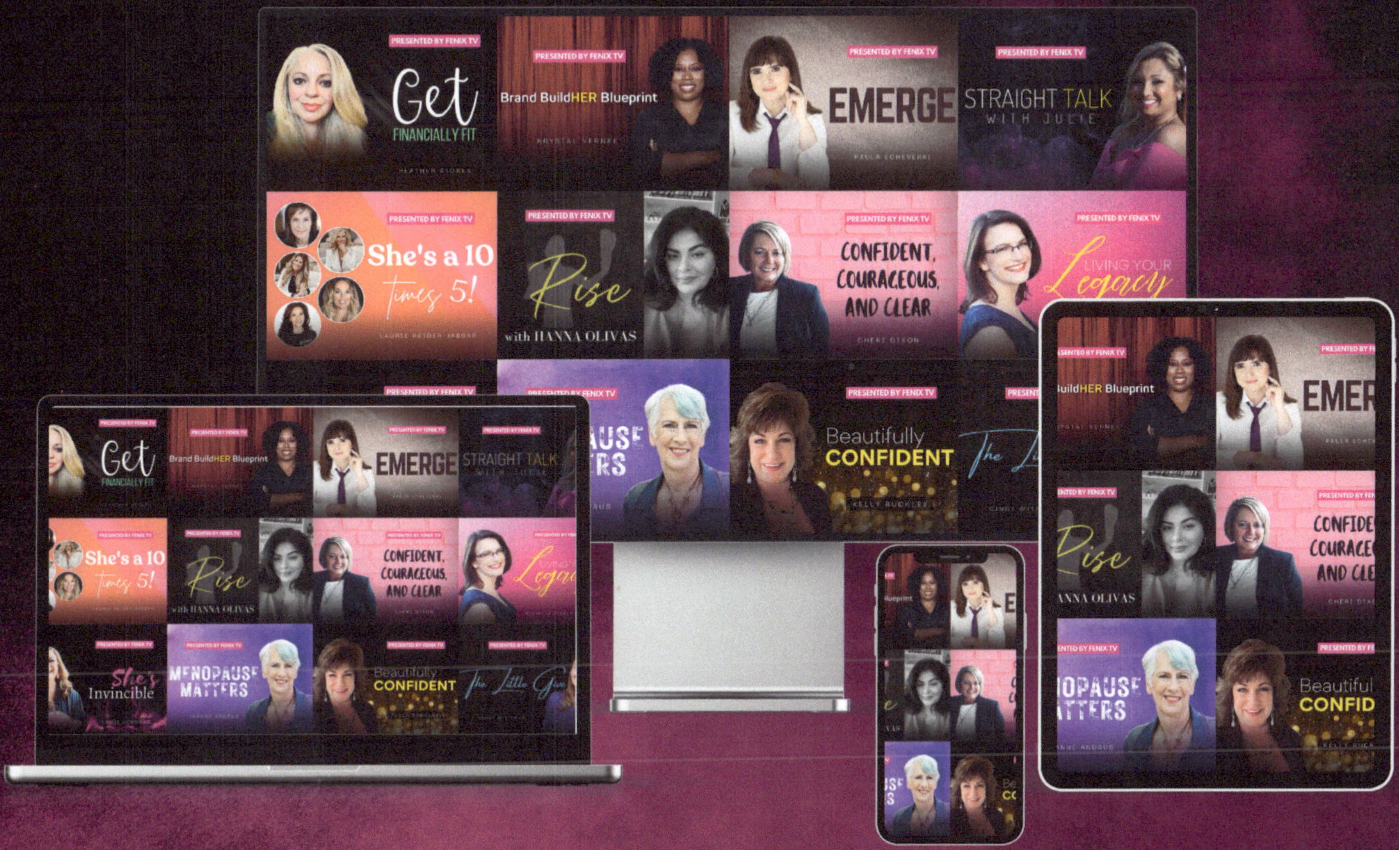

FENIXTV.APP — SIGN UP FOR FREE

HEALTHY MIND, HEALTHY BODY, HEALTHY LIFE

Written By Suzanne Corbo

Please allow me to introduce you to the Corbo Collection, a portfolio of hand-selected, five-star hotels and resorts which focus primarily on health and wellness.

In 2019, I was hired to be part of the opening team at Equinox Hotel in New York City's famed Hudson Yards. Since that time, I have learned so much about the benefits of non-traditional services such as cryotherapy and the infrared sauna. It has fueled my fire to learn more and with my 50th birthday quickly approaching I realize now more than ever the importance of living a healthy lifestyle.

If you are not familiar, cryotherapy is a therapeutic technique that exposes the body to extremely cold temperatures for a very short period; it can go as low as -200 degrees Fahrenheit for two to four minutes max. The benefits include reducing inflammation, managing pain relief, improving athletic performance, accelerating muscle recovery, and increasing metabolism. It is also believed that cryotherapy enhances mental well-being by reducing stress and improving sleep quality.

With similar benefits to cryotherapy, the infrared sauna is another innovative temperature therapy treatment for those that do not like the cold. Unlike conventional saunas that use dry heat to warm the air, infrared lamps create heat in infrared saunas, warming the body directly. Some of the commonly reported health benefits are relaxation and stress relief, detoxification, weight management due to increased calorie burning, relief of muscle aches, joint stiffness, reduced inflammation, fast muscle/injury recovery, improved circulation, and skin health.

I just returned from The Ranch Italy which is also located in Malibu and will be opening in Hudson Valley, New York next spring of 2024. The Ranch offers a unique program which focuses on resetting your mind and body. Guests have thirty days to prepare for their stay and to slowly eliminate caffeine, alcohol, meat, and processed foods. During their visit, they can enjoy two or four hour hikes each day, a daily massage, strength training and yoga classes. The meals are plant based, nutrient dense and vegan. I have done the program twice and never feel better than when I am at The Ranch. I always leave feeling like an unstoppable woman!

For more information on Corbo Collection, please visit www.corbocollection.com.

Get in touch:
www.instagram.com/corbocollection
www.facebook.com/corbocollection

www.corbocollection.com

How Will You Have Time to Run a Business? You're a Mom!

Diana Svensson

Diana Svensson, better known as @Nordicentrepreneur, is a marketing specialist and media mogul who's now featured as an author in the latest SheRises book launch - Women Who Lead, The Future Of Entrepreneurship.

Born in Sweden and raised in six different countries, Diana is a globetrotter who writes about breaking free from society's norms and creating an everyday life that one doesn't need a vacation from. Her inspiration comes from her childhood, which she calls tragicomic, and many of her followers have expressed that they truly recognize themselves in her chapter, which is somewhat about the questions she received while starting her media business.

One of these questions led her to start her podcast 'Women & Entrepreneurship', which Diana recorded with a friend from New Zeeland for a few years before her career took off and there wasn't enough time to continue.

The question was: "But how do you have time to start your own business? You're a mother" to which she simply replied: "Do you ask men the same question?

Diana realized that when speaking publicly in schools around Stockholm, she met many young girls who had ambitions and the drive to become entrepreneurs, but they always seemed to find an excuse related to starting a family. This became a hot topic for her that made her question why men weren't asked the same questions, so she switched her focus from publicly speaking about media trends and startups to coaching other women to fulfill their entrepreneurial dreams.

In the newly released book "Women Who Lead - The Future Of Entrepreneurship" Diana's chapter "The Grey Unicorn" unfolds harsh details about her traumatic childhood, her so-called "friends" who disappeared once she decided to invest in her career, and some important advice she wants to pass on to inspire women to take the leap and break free. The chapter is dedicated to her mother who took her own life back in 2021 when Diana was in the middle of her last studies as a Digital Marketing Specialist.

Today, she has overcome more challenges than ever and started her own media agency HYPE ME where she has a team of handpicked specialists working towards one particular goal - elevating women-owned brands to new heights!

You can contact the team and find out more at: www.hypeme.se
or contact Diana directly at IG handle: @Nordicentrepreneur

Illustration Credit: NAG Atelier

www.dianasvensson.com | www.linkedin.com/in/dianasvensson
www.instagram.com/nordicentrepreneur | www.hypeme.se

The SHE RISES STUDIOS PODCAST

The She Rises Studios podcast is dedicated to empowering women like you to reach their full potential and live their best lives. With inspiring stories, insightful interviews, and practical advice from experts in different industries, our podcast is your go-to source for information, inspiration, and motivation. Join us as we explore topics like:

- Overcoming self-doubt and limiting beliefs
- Building and running a successful business
- Building confidence and Self-esteem
- Navigating career transitions
- Starting and growing a business
- Balancing work and family life
- Improving physical and mental health
- Finding meaning and purpose in life
- So many more

Our guests include successful entrepreneurs, inspiring thought leaders, and everyday women who have overcome challenges and achieved their dreams. Each episode is packed with actionable tips and strategies to help you take your life to the next level.

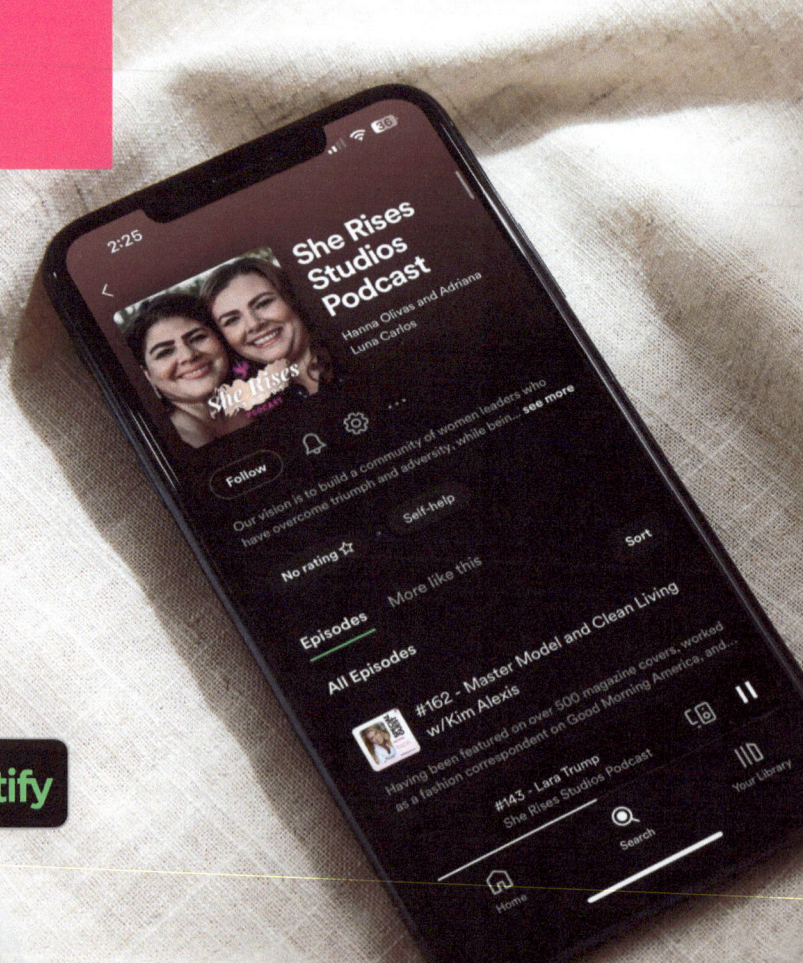

Money Talks: The Importance of Financial Literacy and How It Can Improve Your Life

Financial literacy is the ability to understand and effectively manage one's financial affairs. In today's world, financial literacy is more important than ever before. From credit card debt to retirement planning, the financial decisions we make can have a significant impact on our lives. In this article, we will explore the importance of financial literacy, the benefits of being financially literate, and some practical tips for improving your financial literacy.

Importance of Financial Literacy

Financial literacy is important for several reasons. Firstly, it enables individuals to make informed financial decisions. With a good understanding of financial concepts, individuals can make informed decisions about their investments, budgeting, and spending. They can also avoid financial scams and make better financial choices.

Secondly, financial literacy helps individuals to build wealth. By understanding financial concepts, individuals can take steps to increase their income, save money, and invest wisely. This can help them to achieve their financial goals and build a secure financial future.

Finally, financial literacy is important for the overall health of the economy. When individuals are financially literate, they are more likely to make responsible financial decisions that benefit both themselves and the wider economy.

Benefits of Financial Literacy

The benefits of financial literacy are numerous. Firstly, financially literate individuals are better able to manage their finances. They are more likely to have a budget, save money, and invest wisely. This can help them to achieve their financial goals and build a secure financial future.

Secondly, financially literate individuals are better able to avoid financial scams. With a good understanding of financial concepts, individuals can spot financial scams and avoid being taken advantage of.

Finally, financially literate individuals are more likely to be financially independent. By understanding financial concepts, individuals can take control of their finances and make informed financial decisions. This can help them to build wealth and achieve their financial goals.

Tips for Improving Financial Literacy

Improving your financial literacy doesn't have to be difficult. Here are some practical tips for improving your financial literacy:

1. **Read financial books and articles** - There are many books and articles available on financial topics. Read them to gain a better understanding of financial concepts.
2. **Take a financial literacy course** - Many community colleges and universities offer financial literacy courses. Consider taking one to improve your financial knowledge.
3. **Seek advice from financial professionals** - Financial professionals, such as financial planners and advisors, can provide valuable advice on financial matters.
4. **Use financial apps and tools** - There are many financial apps and tools available that can help you manage your finances and improve your financial literacy.
5. **Practice good financial habits** - Make a budget, save money, and invest wisely. By practicing good financial habits, you will improve your financial literacy over time.

Financial literacy is a vital skill in today's world. It enables individuals to make informed financial decisions, build wealth, and achieve financial independence. By improving your financial literacy, you can take control of your finances and build a secure financial future.

By Adriana Luna Carlos
She Rises Studios

WOMEN IN
BU$INESS

Empowering Emotional Resilience: Practical Techniques for Better Results in Life

BY CHRISTINA ALDAN

It's time to get real about emotions in the workplace. We've all had those days where emotions run high, making it hard to focus on work. Whether it's a personal issue, conflict with a coworker, or feeling overwhelmed, we're still expected to manage our responsibilities in a professional manner. But how can we accomplish that? By hiding in the bathroom stall to silent-cry? That's a useful technique sometimes, but not as a daily strategy. Or by making more workplace rules? That seems to demoralize the company when the rules aren't fairly enforced. Unfortunately, neither of these solutions --hiding nor policing-- can stop emotions from arising in the workplace. The truth is that we can't simply policy emotions out of the workplace. However, we can teach communication skills by empowering people with tools for emotional resilience.

Here are three proven solutions I use to help my clients and mentees get better results in their personal and in their work lives:

1. Mental Health First Aid: Mental health issues are more common than you might think. According to the World Health Organization, one in four people in the world will be affected by mental or neurological disorders at some point in their lives. And they take those issues with them to work, to the grocery, to the mall...wherever they go. This includes conditions such as grief, depression, and anxiety. So, it's likely that someone in your workplace is dealing with a mental health issue right now. Mental Health First Aid is a training certification program that teaches people how to recognize the early signs of a mental health crisis and how to provide support to someone who is experiencing one. By learning these skills, team members can use nuanced phrases to improve communication with someone who may be exhibiting early warning signs of a mental health crisis. Mental Health First Aiders also learn how to help

someone in the midst of a crisis. This, in turn, reduces stress in the workplace. Research has shown that mental health first aid can improve mental health literacy, reduce stigma, and increase confidence in providing support to others (Jorm et al., 2010). Having staff members who are trained to recognize and respond to a person who is struggling demonstrates a supportive workplace culture that values mental health.

Research supports the effectiveness of Mental Health First Aid (MHFA). A study published in the Journal of the American Medical Association found that individuals who received MHFA training had improved knowledge of mental health issues and were more likely to seek help for themselves or others. If you or someone you know would like to be certified in MHFA for Youth or Adults, please contact The Avery Burton Foundation (https://AveryBurtonFoundation.org) to find out how to join an upcoming cohort of learners.

2. Conflict Resolution: Conflict in the workplace is inevitable, but how we handle it can make all the difference. Learning conflict-resolution skills can help you resolve disputes with coworkers in a productive and respectful manner. Conflict resolution involves active listening, empathy, and finding a mutually beneficial solution. By using these skills, you can prevent conflicts from escalating and improve working relationships.
A study published in the International Journal of Conflict Management found that employees who received conflict resolution training had better job satisfaction, lower stress levels, and improved working relationships. So conflict resolution training can improve workplace outcomes. To help people practice these skills in a safe environment with strangers so you don't have to worry about retaliation (because who wants to practice dealing with tough emotions with your boss? Maybe

your boss is the problem!), I recently launched a monthly Leadership Improv Practicum co-facilitated alongside Leslie Martinich, president of the IEEE and international trainer. The Zoom class is spent practicing skills with people from different companies and industries. We role-play actual scenarios from Leslie's 20+ years in engineering leadership to learn leadership skills. Contact me to sign up for our next class (I am @luckygirliegirl and my DM's are open).

3. Emotional intelligence is often defined as the ability to perceive, use, understand, manage, and process emotions. Individuals with high emotional intelligence can recognize their own emotions and those of others. They are able to utilize emotional information to guide thinking and behavior, differentiate between different feelings and appropriately label them, and adapt emotions to the environment. That emotional resilience to overcome the ups and downs of life is the stuff of leaders. A peer-reviewed study published in the Journal of Organizational Behavior revealed that individuals with higher emotional intelligence were more likely to be rated as effective leaders and to exhibit better job performance. Developing emotional intelligence can enhance communication skills, improve relationships, and lead to better decision-making. Self-awareness, self-regulation, motivation, empathy, and social skills are part of the 26 traits involved in emotional intelligence. Mindfulness practices such as meditation or deep breathing exercises are one way to develop emotional intelligence. These

practices can help you become more aware of your own emotions and reactions, which leads to learning how to regulate your emotions more effectively. Another way to develop emotional intelligence is by cultivating empathy). Empathy means you can shift your perspective (https://www.luckygirliegirl.com/is-it-time-for-a-fresh-perspective/) and put yourself in someone else's shoes. Practicing empathy (https://www.luckygirliegirl.com/empathy-superpower-part-1/) allows individuals to shift perspectives and understand the feelings of others, thus fostering stronger relationships and better conflict management skills. Research has demonstrated that emotional intelligence is positively associated with job performance, job satisfaction, and leadership effectiveness (Joseph & Newman, 2010).

Rather than creating rules that ban emotions, let us learn strategies for regulating emotions, building resilience, and assisting individuals in mental health crises. By practicing Mental Health First Aid, Conflict Resolution, and Emotional Intelligence, we can improve our communication skills, build better relationships, and cultivate a supportive workplace culture that values mental health. We can empower ourselves with tools for emotional resilience and become the best versions of ourselves. Even small steps in developing emotional intelligence can have a significant impact on our lives and the world around us.

References:

1. Mental Health First Aid Training for the Public: Evaluation of Effects on Knowledge, Attitudes and Helping Behavior, Anthony F. Jorm, Betty A. Kitchener, Claire M. O'Kearney, Journal of BMC Psychiatry, https://bmcpsychiatry.biomedcentral.com/articles/10.1186/1471-244X-4-9
2. Conflict Resolution Strategies and their Performance: A Study on International Business Negotiations, Svetlana Holt, Leona Tam, International Journal of Business and Management, https://doi.org/10.5539/ijbm.v10n2p239
3. The Importance of Emotional Intelligence in the Workplace: Why It Matters More Than Personality, Ashley M. Guidroz, Dana Joseph, Jennifer L. Moye, Journal of Applied Social Psychology, https://doi.org/10.1111/jasp.12207
4. Griffith, J., & Frieden, J. (2000). Training for conflict resolution: A study of its effectiveness for organizations. International Journal of Conflict Management, 11(1), 32-55, https://www.emerald.com/insight/content/doi/10.1108/eb022834/full/html
5. Joseph, D. L., & Newman, D. A. (2010). Emotional intelligence: An integrative meta-analysis and cascading model. Journal of Applied Psychology, 95(1), 54-8.J, https://www.sciencedirect.com/science/article/pii/S0191886922004226

Christina Aldan
www.abfresiliencyproject.org/community-matters
www.luckygirliegirl.com
@luckygirliegirl everywhere else on the interwebs

Uncovering the Truth - Revealing the Secrets to Genuine and Lasting Healing

Alexa Elbrader

Unleashing the power within, fueling a vision that transcends the confines of the ordinary. Are you ready to embark on a transformative journey, an odyssey of healing and self-discovery? In a world plagued by the shadows of chronic illness and mental strife, the longing to revolutionize the depths of our being becomes an unstoppable force.

My personal journey to health and wholeness has been a tumultuous one with challenges and obstacles that threatened to dampen the flame within. Yet, through it all, an unconquerable spirit emerged, fueled by a deep reservoir of enthusiasm for wellness and a relentless quest for truth. In a world where the secrets of genuine healing are often concealed, hidden behind the veil of the pharmaceutical industry, I made the decision to sever ties and embark on a soul-stirring expedition of my own. Armed with determination and an appetite for knowledge, I ventured into uncharted territories, unearthing the hidden gems of true healing. It was during this expedition that I stumbled upon a revelation that would alter the course of my life - the transformative power of gut health.

What is gut health? It encompasses the overall well-being and optimal functioning of our gastrointestinal (GI) tract, a complex system responsible for digestion, nutrient absorption, immune function and even disease prevention. Maintaining a balance of beneficial bacteria, ensuring proper digestion, and nurturing a strong intestinal barrier are all essential components of a healthy gut. It is the cornerstone of our well-being, a foundation upon which vibrant health is built. It's no exaggeration that the gut operates as our second brain, having formed even before our physical bodies in the womb!

However, not all gut health products are created equal. Enter the Gut Collective product line (created by the company of Xyngular), a revelation that has transformed my life in ways I never thought possible.

Within three days of incorporating these products into my routine, I experienced a life-altering shift. My gut finally began to heal. Fast forward a month in, as stubborn weight melted away, shedding eight pounds from my gut area and inches from my waistline. The Gut Collective's superior products are designed to literally change your body from the inside out. You will see positive changes, feel pain and fatigue subside, and watch your body age in reverse. But the transformation extended far beyond physical changes.

I began noticing astonishing improvement in my mental clarity, moods, and overall well-being. As a result of their effectiveness, it was a natural choice for me to become an X-Brand partner for Xyngular - a company I knew I had to share with the world.

With Xyngular, I discovered a vision for a brighter future that resonated deep within my soul. I aspired to create an environment where individuals could embrace a comprehensive approach to wellness, one that nurtures the mind, body, and spirit. A safe haven where the hopeless find hope, the misunderstood find understanding, and the unheard find their voice.

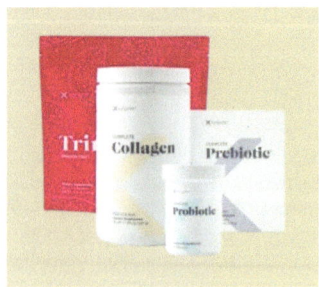

It brings me joy knowing that these aspirations of mine are entirely possible because of what being an X-brand partner means. When you join the team, here are a few of the incredible benefits you can expect:

• A business structure with built-in flexibility. Sign up, share, and earn daily pay all while setting your own schedule. Bonus: we create the marketing material and provide you with your own website!
• A supply of natural plant-based, award-winning supplements that have a 94% success rate.
• A life of adventure–think world travel and 5-star resort accommodations for two in places like Jamaica, Dubai, Europe, etc.
• A role in one of the fastest growing, well-established industries (already at $151.9 BILLION and projected to grow by 8% every year). It's an industry that will never go out of style.
• A willable income - the business you work hard to build can be passed down to those who come after you.

Join me as we explore the intricate dance between gut health and overall well-being. Welcome to a world where vision knows no bounds, where the power to change both our surroundings and ourselves lies within our grasp. Are you ready to embark on this transformative journey? The future awaits, and it is brimming with possibilities.

www.myxyngular.com/en/lexirelbrader | www.facebook.com/lexi.r.elbrader

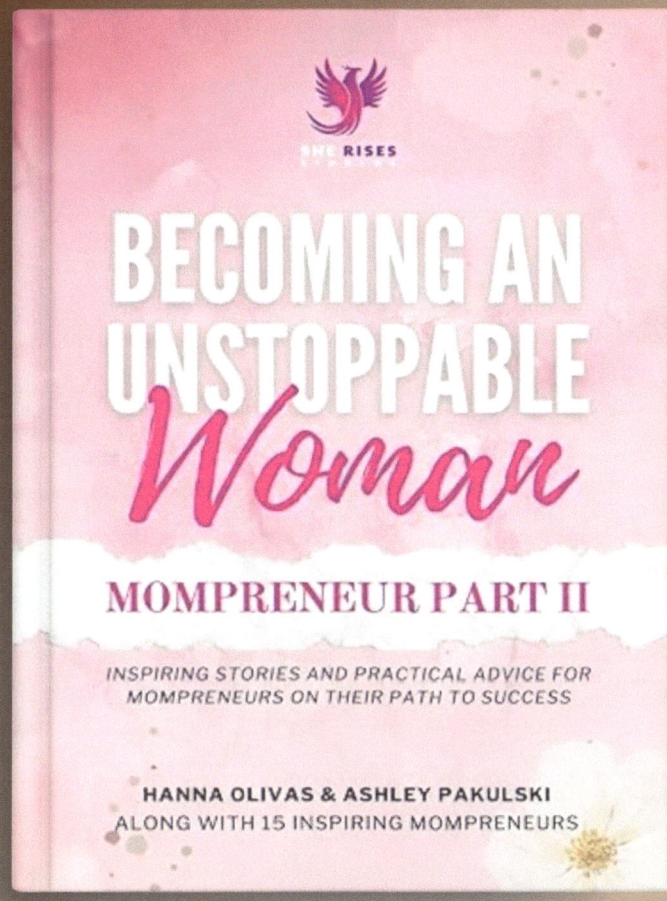

THE POWER OF GRATITUDE: CULTIVATING ABUNDANCE AND WELL-BEING

Gratitude is a universal emotion that can transform our lives and bring abundance and well-being. Derived from the Latin word "gratia," which means grace or gratefulness, gratitude encompasses the appreciation and recognition of the goodness in our lives. It is a conscious acknowledgment of the positive experiences and contributions of others that enrich our existence. I make a conscious effort to practice gratitude and to help others experience appreciation. It is customary for those who know me that I take pleasure in sharing small but memorable tokens of appreciation. For example, our words are powerful. I take time to write thank you cards and motivational messages for others so that an opportunity for reflection and appreciation of the daily life we create becomes evident.

Many have experienced joy in receiving a bouquet or candles to bring light to their lives. Other times, it can be just a simple but honest compliment to remind them how precious they are. I have made gratitude a part of my life's journey because I realized that having an appreciation for all that is it was a sure method for increasing the value of everything and everyone around me. Seeing their expression is what brings tremendous joy to my heart, and this raises my emotional vibration to the highest level. In this article, we will explore the science-backed benefits of practicing gratitude and its impact on our physical and mental health, relationships, and overall life satisfaction. We will also delve into practical ways to cultivate gratitude daily.

The Science of Gratitude

Scientific research has shown that gratitude is strongly associated with greater happiness and well-being. Psychologists like Dr. Robert A. Emmons and Dr. Michael E. McCullough have conducted extensive studies on gratitude, revealing its profound effects on individuals' lives. In one study, participants were asked to write about things they were grateful for each week, while another group focused on daily irritations or neutral events. The findings demonstrated that those who practiced gratitude experienced increased optimism, better overall life satisfaction, and even engaged in healthier behaviors such as regular exercise and fewer visits to physicians.

Dr. Martin E. P. Seligman, a leading researcher in positive psychology, conducted a study in which participants were assigned to write and deliver a letter of gratitude to someone who had never been properly thanked. The results showed an immediate and significant increase in happiness scores, surpassing the impact of other interventions. Gratitude not only benefits the giver and the recipient but also positively affects those who witness acts of appreciation, fostering feelings of warmth and affinity towards both parties.

The Benefits of Gratitude on Mental Health

Cultivating gratitude has a profound impact on our mental health and emotional well-being. Expressing gratitude helps reduce symptoms of depression and anxiety, improves self-esteem, and enhances satisfaction with daily life. By focusing on the positive aspects of our lives, we shift our perspective from what we lack to what we have, fostering a sense of abundance. Gratitude also enables us to build resilience, effectively coping with adversity and cultivating an optimistic attitude.

Gratitude and Physical Health

The benefits of gratitude extend beyond our mental well-being and have a positive impact on our physical health. Studies have shown that individuals who practice gratitude experience fewer aches and pains, report better overall health, and are more likely to engage in proactive behaviors such as regular exercise and attending medical check-ups. Gratitude has been associated with lower blood pressure and increased heart rate variability, a marker of well-being. By fostering a grateful mindset, we can improve our physical health and well-being.

Gratitude and Relationships

Gratitude plays a crucial role in fostering and strengthening our relationships with others. Expressing gratitude towards acquaintances, friends, family, and romantic partners enhances the quality of these relationships. Appreciation acts as a relationship "boost," making individuals feel more positive toward one another and facilitating open communication. Managers who express gratitude towards their employees often find that it motivates them to work harder, increasing productivity. Gratitude creates a positive cycle of appreciation and reciprocity, strengthening social bonds.

Cultivating an Attitude of Gratitude

Gratitude is a quality that can be cultivated and developed over time. By practicing gratitude regularly, we can enhance its positive effects on our lives. Here are some practical ways to incorporate gratitude into our daily routines:

1. Keep a Gratitude Journal

Maintain a gratitude journal where you write down the things you are grateful for each day. Reflect on the blessings, big and small, that you have experienced. This practice helps shift your focus to the positive aspects of your life, increasing your awareness of the abundance around you.

2. Write Thank-You Notes

Express your gratitude to others by writing thank-you notes or emails. Take the time to acknowledge and appreciate the impact they have had on your life. This simple act of gratitude strengthens relationships and fosters a sense of connection and appreciation.

3. Practice Mindfulness and Meditation

Incorporate gratitude into your mindfulness or meditation practice. Focus on the present moment and intentionally cultivate gratitude for the simple joys and blessings in your life. This practice helps shift your mindset to one of appreciation and contentment.

4. Count Your Blessings

Set aside time each week to reflect on your blessings. Write down three to five things you are grateful for and reflect on the positive sensations associated with those experiences. By consciously counting your blessings, you reinforce the habit of gratitude and develop a more optimistic outlook on life.

5. Share Acts of Kindness

Engage in acts of kindness and generosity towards others. By spreading positivity and gratitude, you create a ripple effect of gratitude and compassion in your community. Small gestures of appreciation, such as saying thank you or offering a helping hand, can have a significant impact on others' lives.

Gratitude is a powerful tool that can significantly enhance our overall well-being and abundance. By practicing gratitude, we cultivate a positive mindset, improve our mental and physical health, strengthen relationships, and increase our overall life satisfaction. Incorporating gratitude into our daily lives is a simple yet transformative practice that allows us to recognize the goodness in our lives and connect with something larger than ourselves. So, let us embrace gratitude and unlock its transformative power to live a life filled with abundance and joy.

"Gratitude is the healthiest of all human emotions. The more you express gratitude for what you have, the more likely you will have even more to express gratitude for." - Zig Ziglar

References

www.chopra.com/articles/use-gratitude-to-cultivate-abundance-mindset
www.mayoclinichealthsystem.org/hometown-health/speaking-of-health/can-expressing-gratitude-improve-health
www.psychologytoday.com/us/blog/what-mentally-strong-people-dont-do/201504/7-scientifically-proven-benefits-of-gratitude
www.positivepsychology.com/gratitude-appreciation/
www.timesofindia.indiatimes.com/readersblog/divine-badass/the-magic-of-gratitude-and-the-way-to-make-it-a-part-of-our-life-44766/ https://www.nytimes.com/2023/06/08/well/mind/gratitude-health-benefits.html

Lorilet Monegro, EdD, M.S., CCC-SLP, TSHH-BE
Bilingual Speech Language Pathologist
Terapeuta Bilingue/Fonoaudiologa

Dr. Lorilet Monegro is a pediatric speech and language pathologist focusing on bilingual Spanish/English language development and disorders. She is based in Westchester County, New York. Dr. Monegro holds a Bachelor of Science in Speech-Language Pathology and Audiology from New York University and a Master of Science in Speech-Language Pathology from Long Island University — Brooklyn Campus. She completed The Bilingual Extension Institute program for speech-language pathologists under the direction of Dr. Cate Crowley from Columbia University.

www.ingramcontent.com/pod-product-compliance
Lightning Source LLC
Chambersburg PA
CBHW041603120626
46551CB00002B/292